Filling Station
Collectibles

with Price Guide

Rick Pease

77 Lower Valley Road, Atglen, PA 19310

DEDICATION

This book is dedicated to my wife Gloria Pease and all the wives who have had to put up with rusty gasoline pumps, greasy oil cans, and dirty old signs and never complained—even when we cleaned them in the kitchen sink.

ACKNOWLEDGEMENTS

I would like to take this opportunity to thank the people who allowed me to take pictures of their collectibles. My thanks to Kyle Moore, Howard Clayburn, Charles Middleton, Roy Reed, Sonya Stenzler, Mike Worley, Ron Carey, Barry Baker, David Anderson, David Wallace, Brad Lago, George and Melba Rook, Layne Christenson, Norm Rubenstein, Paul Durall, Mike O'Hern, and many more who were so kind to let me photograph their collectibles. Thanks to all.

Published by
Schiffer Publishing Ltd.
77 Lower Valley Road
Atglen, PA 19310
Please write for a free catalog.
This book may bepurchased from the publisher.Please include $2.95 postage.
Try your bookstore first.

 CONTENTS

A Note On Price Ranges

The price ranges provided after each item are meant only as guidelines, and they should help you to determine a general estimate of current market prices. However, collectors must be aware that many factors influence prices, including condition of the item and place of purchase. All collectors must use their best judgment!

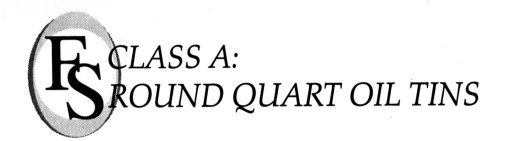

CLASS A:
ROUND QUART OIL TINS

Round quart oil cans were introduced around 1932. All major and independent oil companies found another product to advertise through the use of logos. Most of the early logos were very colorful and picturesque, although some were very simple. The following cans are from approximately 1932 to the present. Quart cans were also used to package anti-freeze and oil treatment.

WIL-FLO Motor Oil, $65 - 75
Golden SHELL Motor Oil, $75 - 90
Invader $30-35

LION HEAD Motor Oil, $75 - 110
Oilzum Motor Oil, $50 - 65
Indian Premium, $100 - 110

Indian Motorcycle Oil, $110 - 125
HIPPO Oil, $145 - 195
FRIGIDTEST Anti-freeze, $160 - 180

20-W Motor Oil, $40 - 45
EN-AR-CO Motor Oil, $100-125
SINCLAIR Motor Oil, $25 - 40

NOURSE Heavy Duty Oil, $35 - 40
WOW Motor Oil, $25 - 30
FREEDOM Motor Oil, $25 - 35

GRAND CHAMPION, $475 - 500
RARNSDALL Motor Oil, $140 - 150
PENRECO Motor Oil, $25 - 35

Penn Drake HI-COMPRESSION, $25 - 35
Oilzum Motor Oil, 90 - 130
KOLDPRUF Anti-freeze, $10 - 15

PENNSYLVANIA Motor Oil, $150 - 165
PENN FRANKLIN Motor Oil, $25 - 35
ParaPride Motor Oil, $50 - 75

HARRIS OILS, $20 - 25
NOURSE Motor Oil, $20 - 30
PENNZOIL, $55 - 60

ARCHER Lubricants, $55 - 65
FALCON Motor Oil, $10 - 15
SKYWAY Motor Oil, $250 - 275

PARA-FIELD Motor Oil, $110 - 12
Mobiloil "BB", $80 - 90
Pennzoil $50-65

HD Colonel Drake, $15 - 25
AVIATION Engine Oil, $40 - 65
Certified FLEET-WING Motor Oil, $35 - 40

7

WELCH Guaranteed Motor Oil, $45 - 60
Road Runner Motor Oil, $25 - 40

BISONOIL, $125 - 155
Phillips Trop-Artic, $150 - 175
PENN BEE Motor Oil, $150 - 175

QUAKER STATE Racing Motor Oil, $10 - 20
Engine Aid Engine Treatment, $15 - 25
INVADER All-Temp Motor Oil, $20 - 30

CITIES SERVICE KOLDPRUF, $30 - 40
MARATHON V.E.P. Motor Oil, $65 - 80
PRX Racing Motor Oil, $35 - 45

FREEDOM PERFECT Motor Oil, $100 - 110
HEART O PENNSYLVANIA, $30 - 45
QUAKER CITY Motor Oil, 70 - 80

Penn Drake HD Motor Oil, $25 - 35
Phillips 66 PREMIUM, $25 - 35
Mobiloil, $25 - 35

BUICK Rear Axle Lubricant, $15 - 30
STERLING Motor Oil, $25 - 35

Penn Drake Motor Oil, $25 - 35
PENN CHAMP Motor Oil, $10 - 15
KENDALL 2000 Mile Oil, $25 - 35

Maxoil Special Cylinder Lubricant, $40 - 55
ARROW Lubricant, $40 - 50
Superol Motor Oil, $20 - 35

HUSKY Heavy Duty Motor Oil, $375 - 450

AirRace Motor Oil, $150 - 175
HyVIS Motor Oil, $10 - 15
GOLDEN LEAF Motor Oil, $15 - 25

PENN-WAVE Motor Oil, $60 - 75
Atlantic Motor Oil, $75 - 85
M F A HEAVY DUTY, $8 - 12

JOHNSON Motor Oil, $110 - 130
ACE HIGH Motor Oil, $260 - 325
GENUINE Harley-Davidson OIL, $40 - 60

Shamrock Motor Oil, $60 - 85   Stay-Ready Fluid, $120 - 140

SKYDROL Hydraulic Fluid, $60 - 75

Wings, $35 - 40

Penn Glenn, $30 - 45

Pennstate Motor Oils, $30 - 45
Liberty Gear Lube, $20 - 25

Red Hat Motor Oil, $175 - 250

Gold Lube Motor Oil, $45 - 65

Indian Penn Chief, $125 - 175

Wareco Penn Motor Oil, $120 - 140

DOUBLE EAGLE Motor Oil, $10 - 15
NOCO Motor Oil, $10 - 15
CRUISER Pennsylvania Motor Oil, $130 - 160

Mohawk Chieftain Motor Oil, $150 - 200
Aero Mobiloil, $75 - 95
PENNTROLEUM Motor Oil, $70-80

MOORE'S C-75 Motor Oil, $15 - 20
Thompson Products Aerotype, $64 - 85
Mother Penn Motor Oil, $40 - 55

TEXAS STAR Motor, $45 - 65
CASPAR, $90 - 120

EN-AR-CO Motor Oil, $100 - 125
TEXACO Motor Oil, $45 - 65

Panhandle Refining Company PANOLENE Motor Oil, $125 - 150
Panhandle PANOLENE Motor Oil (Red Can), $125 - 150

FARGO AERO Motor Oil, $160 - 190
Old Dutch Motor Oil, $150 - 180
CROZOIL Motor Oil, $160 - 190

Hy-Flash Motor Oil, $155 - 195

Early Bird, $75 - 125

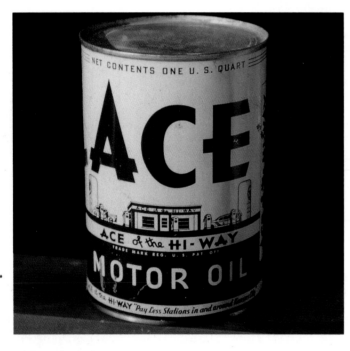

ACE Motor Oil, $195 - 245

Gargoyle Gold, $45 - 70

Barnsdall Motor Oil, $50 - 75

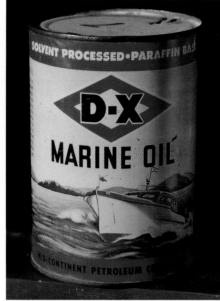

D-X Marine Oil, $95 - 160

Mohawk Chieftain, $115 - 165

Five Point Motor Oil, $125 - 160

Zerolube Winter Motor Oil, $65 - 95

Motor Life Oil, $60 - 75

Kendall 2000 Mile Oil, $65 - 75
Falcon Motor Oil, $10 - 15

Welch Guaranteed, $250 -275
Lucky Strike Motor, $150 -175
Marquette Motor Oil, $175 - 250
Skelly Motor Oil, $40 - 55

Phillips 66 Motor, $180 -225

Lion Head Motor Oil 90 - 140

Spinner Motor Oil, $125 -140

Penn-Bee Motor Oil, $130 -160

Safety Penn Motor, $86 - 100

Farmer's Union, $175 -200

Phillips Trop-Artic, $90 - 130

Three RRR's, $260 -280

Frontier Lube, $125 -150

FILM-X Motor Oil

ACE HIGH Motor Oil, $260-325

TIOPOET Motor Oil, $275 -350

Polly Penn Motor Oil, $800 -975

CLASS B:
FIVE-GALLON OIL CANS

The tin five-gallon oil container was primarily used in industry, farming, retail stores, etc. These containers were used from the teens to the late 1950s.

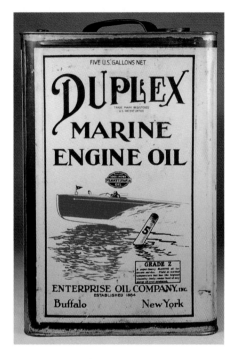

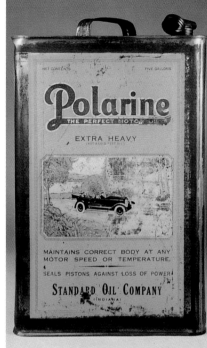

Duplex Marine, $275 - 350

Polarine Extra Heavy, $375 -450

Travelene Motor Oil, $40 - 45

En-ar-co Motor Oil, $40 - 65

Atlantic Motor Oil, $30 - 40

Polarine, $390 - 475

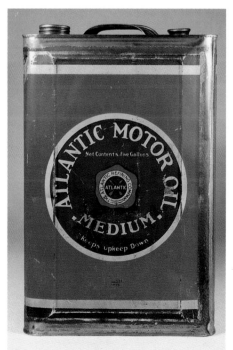

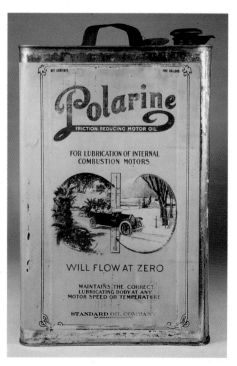

Gargoyle Mobiloil "A", $40 - 65

Zerolene, Zero Cold Test, $150 - 210

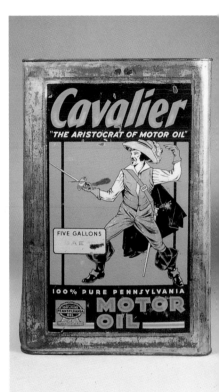

Cavalier Motor Oil, $190 - 275

French Auto Oil, $375 -450

Pennzoil Motor Oil, $20 - 30

En-Ar-Co Motor Oil, $140 -185

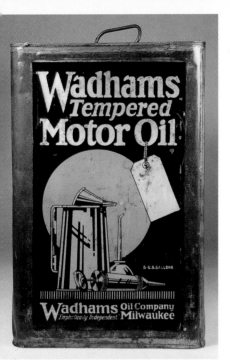

Wadhams Tempered Motor Oil, $120 - 145

Penn City Motor Oil, $110 -145

Booster 100% Pure, $65 - 80

Duplex Motor Oil, $280 -340

Nourse Oils, $100 - 175

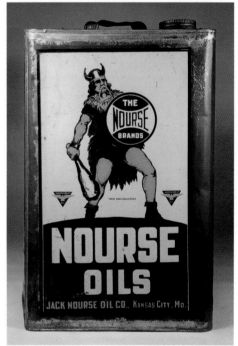

HUDSON MOTOR OIL, $300 - 360

STANARD OF LOUISIANA, $125 - 175

CLASS C: MISCELLANEOUS ITEMS

Miscellaneous advertising items, from pin backs, signs, dinnerware, and air compressors to gas pumps, provided ways for each and every company to get its name in the public eye.

Wolf's Head Banks, $18 - 22 each
Hudsonite Clutch Compound, $10 - 16 each

One-qt. Valvoline Motor Oil, $100 - 110

Mobiloil Rack & Cans, $375 -450

Globe Lubricant, $30 - 35   Sinclair Lith O Line, $10 - 15
Trojan Grease, $15 - 20   Sunoco Motor Cup Grease, $15 - 20
Wolf's Head Lube, $15 - 20   Richlube Lubricant, $15 - 25

Five-qt. Havoline Motor Oil, $20 - 25
Five-qt. Quaker State Motor Oil, $20 - 25
DeLuxe Quaker State, $15 - 20
CORECO Motor Oil, $20 - 25
Duplex Outboard Motor Oil, $70 - 85

Firestone Spark Plugs display case, $160 - 180   Marathon Tire Tin Sign, $650 - 800

Pure as Gold Wheel Bearing Grease with picture of the Pep Boys,
$20 - 25
Motor-Kleen, $10 - 15
Indian Head Brake Fluid, $8 - 10
Quick Tune-up, $10 - 12

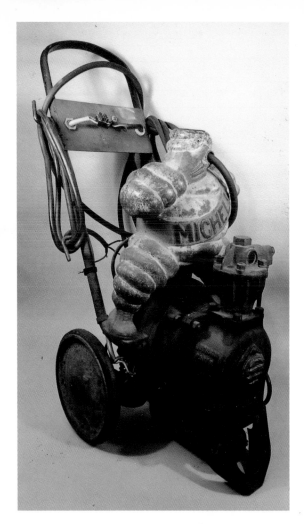

Michelin Man Riding Air Compressor, $1600 -1800

Michelin Man Riding Compressor (very early), $1200 - 1500

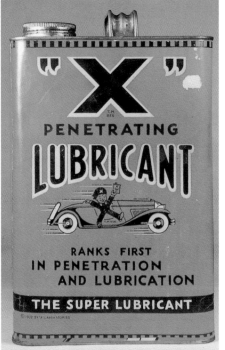

Freedom Grease (10 lb), $15 - 25
Duplex Gear Grease, $35 - 45

"X" Penetrating Lubricant
(ca. 1932), $25 - 45

Nevr-Dull Aircraft Polish, $25 - 35
Parrot Polish, 1 pt., $25+
Parrot Polish, 1/2 pt. 25+

Pure as Gold (5 lb) with picture of the Pep Boys, $50 - 65
Gree-Soff Automobile Soap, $60 - 85
Sambo Axle Grease, Nourse Oil Co. $40 -55

Whiz Cup Grease (51b), $45
Whiz Gear-Lite (10 lb), $70 - 85
Whiz Cup Grease (5 lb), $60

One-qt. Conoco Separator Oil with Minute Man, $450 - 525
One-qt. Nourse Oil Co., $15 - 20
Kant-Rust Motor Tune-Up, $20 - 25

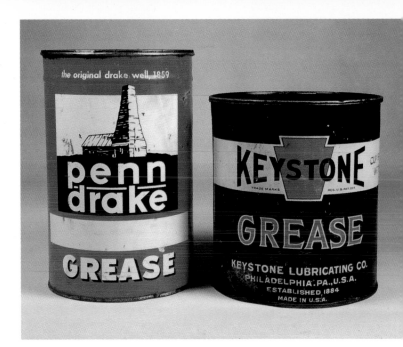

Michelin Tire Patch Box, $250 - 275

Penn Drake Grease, $15+
Keystone Grease Can, $15+

Pennzoil, 10 lb., $15 - 25
Ever-Flow Anti-Freeze, $30 -70
Polarine Transmission Lubricant (very early),
  $30 - 45

Duplex Gear Grease $115 - 140
Trop-Artic Motor Oil "Satisfies from Pole to Pole" (ca. 1910), $90 -
110
Whiz Metal Polish, $30 - 45
Whiz Auto Top Dressing (very early), $45 - 60

Pennzoil Motor Grease, $40 - 50

1918 Blue Book with Michelin advertizing, $100 - 120

Mobil Horse Ashtray, $150 - 200

Champion Dependable Spark Plugs (counter-top display), $175 - 225

Public Telephone, small porcelain, $150 - 225

Texaco early waxed cardboard, $60-80

Texaco Upper Cylinder Lubricant bank, $45 - 50
Havoline Motor Oil bank, $30 - 35
Texaco Sky Chief bank, $90 - 110

Texaco Transmission can, $15 - 20
Conoco Tunes It can, $15 - 20
Conoco Outboard Motor Oil, $15 - 20

Casite painted, tin display rack, $150 - 175

Very early Havoline Cup Motor Grease, $110 - 140

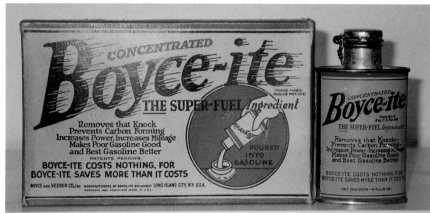

Boyce-its Super Fuel early fuel additive, $40 - 60

'Custom-Made' Havoline Motor Oil, Imperial Quart, $60 -70
Red Indian Aviation Motor Oil, Imperial Quart, $120 - 135
Texaco Motor Oil, Imperial Quart, $60 - 70

Early Texaco Home Lubricant display
with cans, $210 - 240

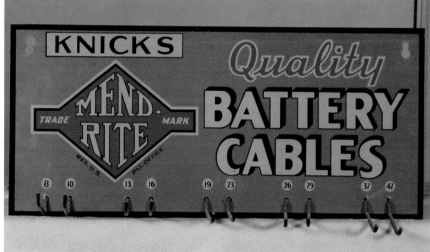

Knicks Mend-Rite Battery Cables, $40 - 65

Oilzum Motor Oil two-sided swing sign, $145 - 180

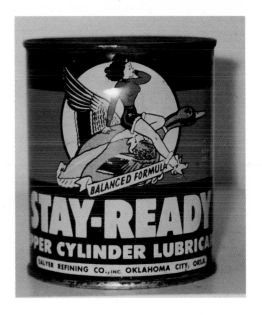

Stay-Ready Upper Cylinder Lubricant, $100 - 125

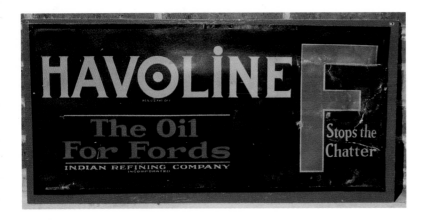

Havoline, Indian Refining Company Cardboard, self-framed in tin, 1918, $225 - 260

Willard Cables and Accessories painted tin, $40 - 60

Texaco Road Map holder (early), $145 - 200

Price Sign, two-sided porcelain (Bowser 1926), very rare. Numbers can be replaced, $195 - 250

Havoline Waxfree Motor Oil small two-sided price tags, $75 - 95

Protect Our Good Name small one-sided porcelain, $125 - 175

No Smoking, porcelain, $140 - 165

Women's Room, very rare, porcelain, dated 1931, $175 - 225

Micro Lube painted tin for oil rack, $80 - 110

Shell Globe Face, 15-inch, for metal-band globe, no pricing

Marathon oil lubster sign, early, painted tin, $110 - 140

Perfection Oil sign, painted tin, $110 - 140

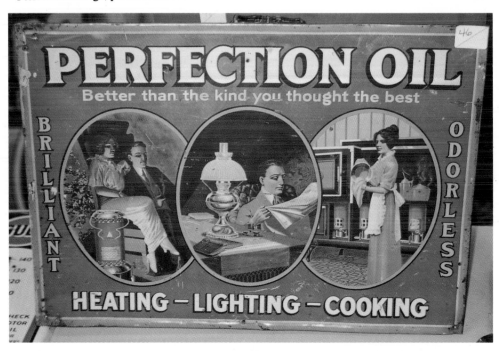

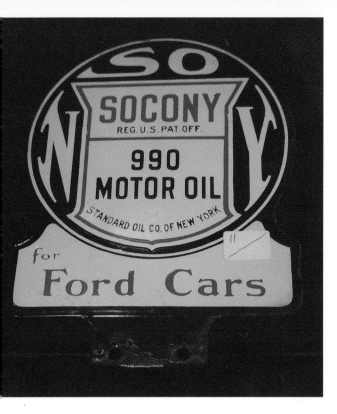

Socony 990 Motor Oil lubster sign, $175 - 225

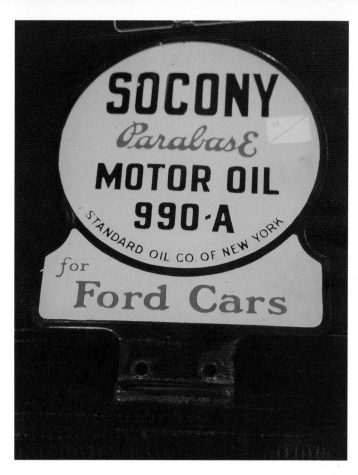

Socony Parabase Motor Oil 990-A lubster sign, $175 - 255

Wayne 866 Clock-Face Pump , $1850 -2450

AVIO Motor Oil, embossed, painted tin, $375 - 400

Cleanzum hand cleaner, no price available

Cleanzum hand cleaner, no price available

Hancock, No Smoking, Stop Motor, $275 - 300

Air and water pump, no pricing available

Shell Station picture, one-of-a-kind, porcelain,
no pricing available

United Service Motors, small, neon, $1600-2850

Rare Standard Oil Company oil lubster sign, porcelain, No Accidents, no pricing available

Associated Gasoline, two-sided, porcelain, $175 - 240

Sunoco Motor Oil Stand, early, $675 - 800

Gargoyle Mobiloil 'E' lubster sign, porcelain, $225 - 250

Super-Shell Ethyl, one-piece, $750 - 850

Trash can, porcelain, $165 - 195

Shell toy truck, early, no pricing available

Marble Rock Michelin Tires, early, painted tire sign, $95-140

French Auto Oil, painted tin, $175 - 200

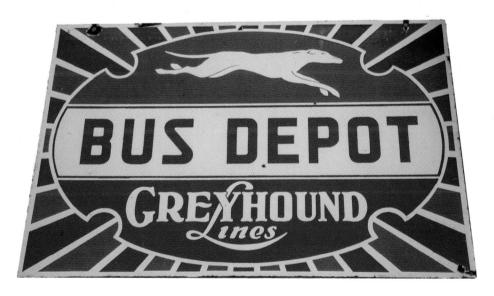

Greyhound Bus Depot sign, early, no pricing available

Welch-Penn Motor Oil, painted tin, $155 - 170

Welch Motor Oil, painted tin, $175 - 200

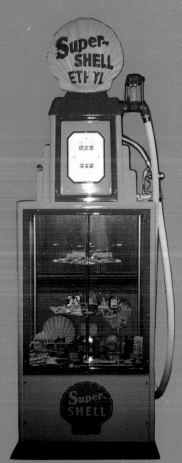

Bowes Tire Service, $140 - 175

Shell, Wayne showcase pump, no pricing available

Welch Motor Oils, small sign, $175 - 250

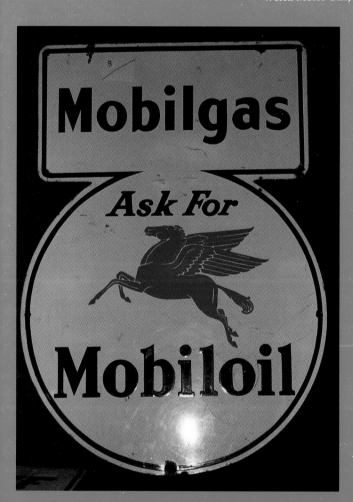

Mobilgas Mobiloil, painted tin sign, $150 - 275

Whitaker Battery Cables, $45 -60
Universal Batteries, $90 - 125
Top Quality ISO VIS Motor Oil painted tin, $125 - 155

Marathon Motor Oils, early painted tin, $1100 - 1250

Indian Gasoline globe, one-piece, etched, $4000 - 5200

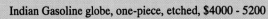

Small Gu1f globe, plastic, with light from the 1950s, $150 175

Early Havoline Oil sign, painted, $175 - 225

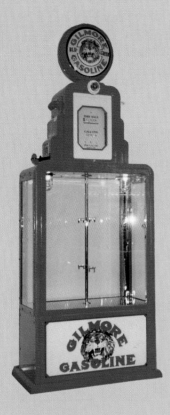

Gilmore Showcase Pump, no price available

Texas Star Globe, no price available

Texaco display, no pricing

Miscellaneous display, no pricing

Miscellaneous display, no pricing

Miscellaneous display, no pricing

Another nice display, no pricing

Texaco dishes: a custard bowl, $45 - 65, a cereal bowl, $45 - 65, an egg cup, $75 - 90, and a dessert bowl, $50 - 65

Texaco dishes: a cup and saucer, $80 -110, a bread dish, $45 - 55, and a dinner plate, $50 - 65

Texaco dishes: an ashtray, $90 - 110, and a match holder, $190 - 200

Texaco Ashtray, 50th Anniversary, $65 - 80

Texaco dishes: a coffee mug, $50 - 60, and a very rare shaving mug, no pricing available

Texaco bear decals, $90 - 100/set

ECO tire meter wall mount, $250 -300

Havoline can, small, $55 - 60
Havoline can, large, $50 - 55

Texaco advertisement, 1931, $60 - 75

Foreground: 1949 Austin Path-Finder peddle car, $3800 - 4000
Background: 1914 Bouser Stoke with globe attachment, $1250 - 1500

Five-gallon Fry Visible gas pump (without globe and sign), $1950 - 2380

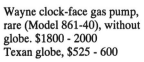

Ten-gallon Fry gas pump, with reproduction globe, $1500 - 1700

Wayne clock-face gas pump, rare (Model 861-40), without globe. $1800 - 2000
Texan globe, $525 - 600

Scottie Dog Lamp, 1931, without shade, $375 - 400 (Please notice the word 'LISTEN' at the base of the lamp)
Lamp shade, 75th Anniversary, $100 - 125
Scottie dog pin-back, $150 - 165
Dallas, Texas Fair, Texaco pin-back, dated 1908, $300 - 350

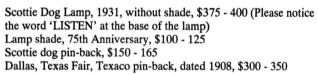

Twin computer gas pumps (reproduction globes), $1550 - 1800

Bennett computer gas pump,
1950s (reproduction globe),
$850 - 1000

Bennett computer gas pump,
1950s, (reproduction globe),
$850 - 1000

Gilbert-Barker ten-gallon
gas pump (reproduction globe),
$1500 - 1800

Bennett computer gas pump, 1950s,
(reproduction globe), $850 - 1000

Bowser clock-face pump
(reproduction globe), $1650 -
1800

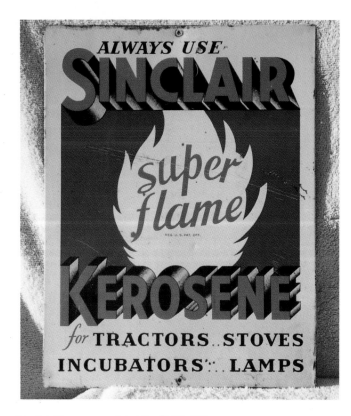

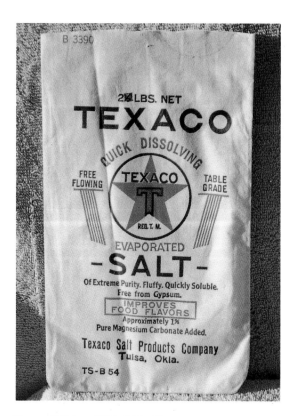

Sinclair Kerosene, painted tin, $165 -180

Texaco Salt bag, 1929, $45 - 55

Texaco Diesel Chief globe in ripple body (single lens) 1350 - 1400

Badger 66 three-piece globe, no pricing available

Texaco Upper Cylinder Lubricant (the glass jar is the oldest), $25 - 110

Texaco Service Oil Co. thermometer, small, $55 -60

Gulf Screw Worm Killer, $20 - 25
Quick Action Gulf Spray, $20 - 25

Texaco Roof Cement, $55 - 90

Fisk tire holder with tire, $150 - 175

Fisk advertisement, a desk light, very early, $450 - 600

Tin two-gallon oil containers came in every shape and size.
They were used from the teens to the 1950s. They also had some
very interesting graphics to catch the public eye.

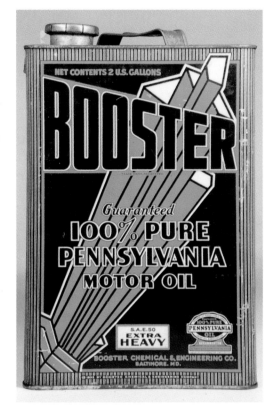

Booster Pennsylvania Motor Oil,
$35 - 50

Film-X Motor Oil, $20 - 35

Mountain State Motor Oil, $40 - 60
Penguin Oil, $120 - 130

Defender Motor Oil, $20 - 30

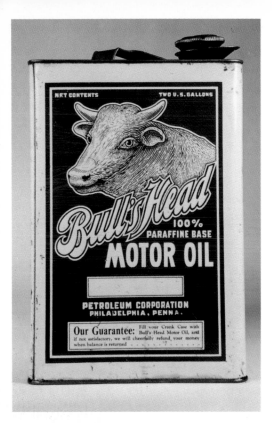

Bull's Head Motor Oil, $130 - 150

Eagle Motor Oil, $175 - 200

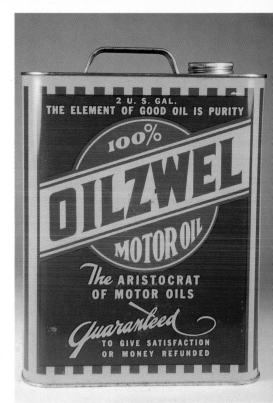

Oilzwel Motor Oil, $25 - 30

Capitol Motor Oil, $40 - 50

Penn-Wave Motor Oil, $30 - 35

Primus Motor Oil, $140 - 160
Grand Champion, $125 - 140

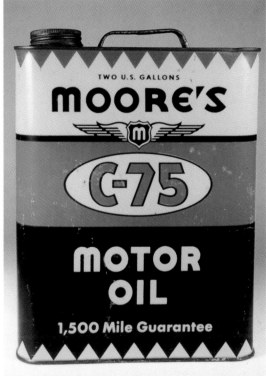

Moore's C-75 Motor Oil, $30 - 80

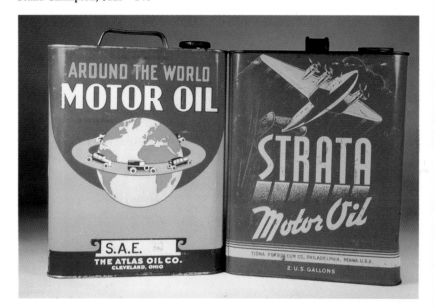

Around the World Motor Oil, $90 -110
Strata Motor Oil, $100 - 115

Green Ray Motor Oil, $145 - 190
Pennsylvania Penn Pool Motor Oil, $150 -175

Penn's All American Motor Oil, $80 - 95
Pep Boys Motor Oil, $190 - 220

Penn Airliner Motor Oil, $125 -135
Ocean Liner Motor Oil, $130 - 150

Economy Motor Oil, $80 - 90
Capital Parlube Motor Oil, $160 - 180

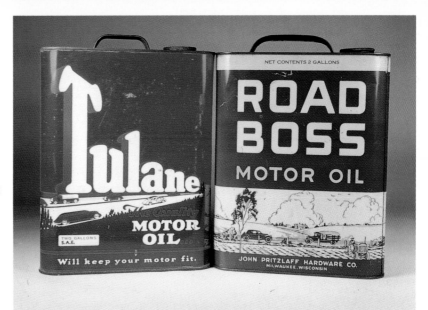

Tulane Motor Oil, $90 - 110
Road Boss Motor Oil, $100 - 115

Sky-High Motor Oil, $120 - 135
Fleetwood Motor Oil, $100 - 125

Motor Oil, Dependable Lubrication for your Motor, $40 - 65
Super Refined AERO Eastern Motor Oil, $125 - 130

Pennsyline Motor and Tractor Oils, $70 - 95
Red Bell Motor Oil, $40 - 60

Pure as Gold Motor Oil, the Pep Boys, $200 - 225
Defender Motor Oil, $50 - 85

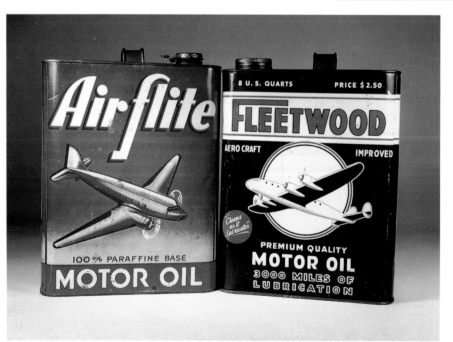

Air Flite Motor Oil, $80 - 95
Fleetwood Motor Oil, $85 - 95

Midland Motor Oil, $60 -85
Tomahawk Motor Oil, $40 - 60

Red Top Motor Oil, $40 -60
Renown Motor Oil, $60 - 75

Traffic Motor Oil, $30 -40
Cruiser Pennsylvania Motor Oil, $45 - 75

Archer Lubricants, $60 -75
Ocean Lines Motor Oil, $110 - 125

Zeppelin Motor Oil, $190 - 210
Penn Trump Motor Oil, $140 - 160

Warren-Teed Motor Oil, $25 - 45
Tankar Special Motor Oil, $30 - 45

Glenwood Motor Oil, $60 - 75
Empire State Motor Oil, $40 - 60

Thorobred Motor Oil, $40 - 65
Bonded Motor Oil, $80 - 110

American Motor Oil, $80 - 110
Penn City Motor Oil, $70 - 80

Rocket Motor Oil, $65 - 75
Nourse Oil Co., $70 - 80

Lubrite Motor Oil, $30 - 45
Silver Shell Motor Oil, $25 - 30

Uncas Motor Oil, $40 - 60
Pennsylvania Motor Oil, $85 - 90

Oneida Motor Oil, $80 - 90
Sturdy Motor Oil, $20 - 40

Sturdy Motor Oil, $45 - 55
Lord Calvert Auto Oil, $80 - 100

Many Miles Motor Oil, $160 - 200
Many Miles Transmission Oil, $120 - 140

Penn Leader Motor Oil, $45 - 70
Infallible Motor Oil, $40 - 60

Pilot Motor Oil, $40 - 60
Your Friend Motor Oil, $25 - 35

Bison Motor Oil, $90 - 110
Bull's Head Motor Oil, $85 - 95

Capitol Motor Oil, $35 - 55

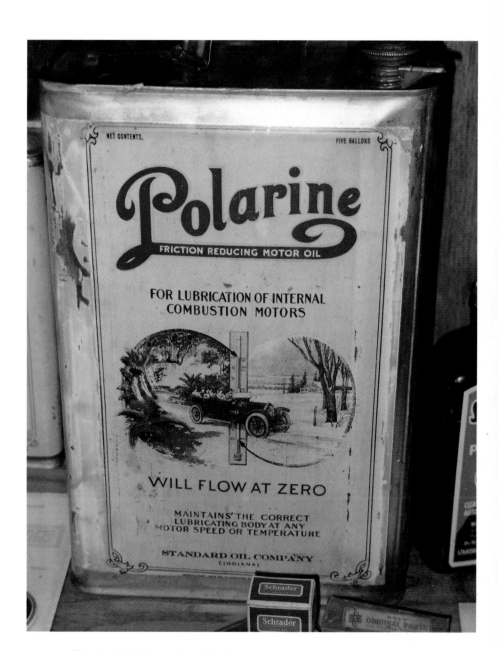

Polarine, Will Flow at Zero, $725 - 850

Pennsylvania Motor Oil, $50 - 75

ℱＳ CLASS E: ONE-GALLON OIL CANS

Tin one-gallon oil cans were used from the teens to the late 1960s. They were utilized in the industrial community as well as for personal use. They also used colors and graphics to sell their products and names.

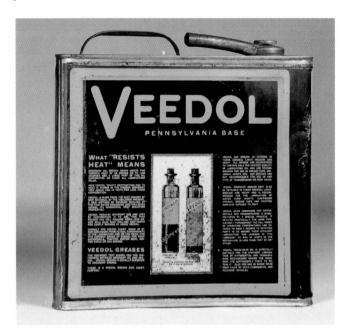

Veedol Pennsylvania Base, $40 - 45

Pennzoil Safe Lubrication, $40 - 55

Invader Oil, $375 - 450

Keystone Penetrating Oil, $30 - 45

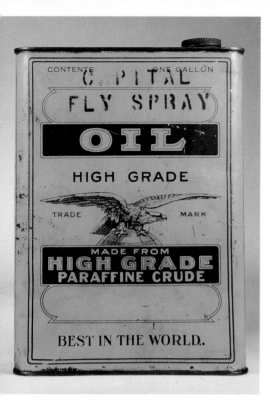

Capital Fly Spray Oil, High Grade, $45 -75

Freedom 'FOWCO' Motor Oil, $60 - 75

Zerolene, Medium, $25 - 35

Tagolene, $30 - 35

Freedom Motor Oil, $25 - 45

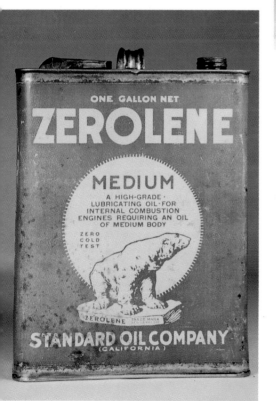

Butler Oil Sales Co., Pennsylvania Bruin, $40 - 85

Navy Motor Oil, $40 - 60

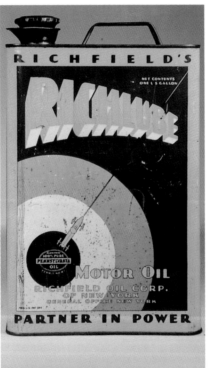

Richfield's Richlube Motor Oil, $70 - 85

Kendall Motor Oil, $45 - 55

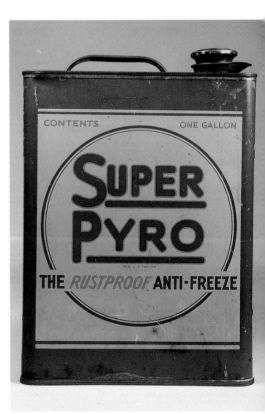

Super Pyro Anti-Freeze, $35 - 45

Tiolene Motor Oil, $40 - 60

Pennzoil Safe Lubrication, $250 -300

Nourse Motor Oil, $275 - 300

Packard Chassis Lubricator Oil, $150 - 175

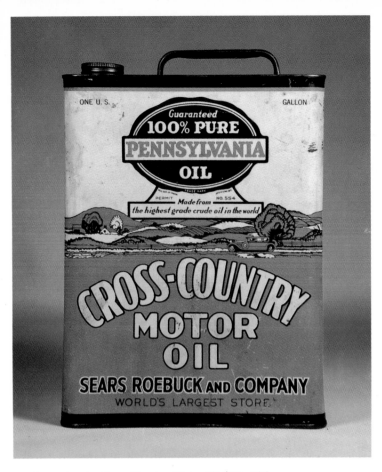

Pennsylvania, Cross-Country Motor Oil, $75 - 125

Approved Red Hat Motor Oil, $900 -1200

Polarine Motor Lubrication (Standard Oil Company), $1000 - 1450

Agalion Motor Oil, $375 - 425

M & W Gas & Oil Co. Better Oil, $875 -1000

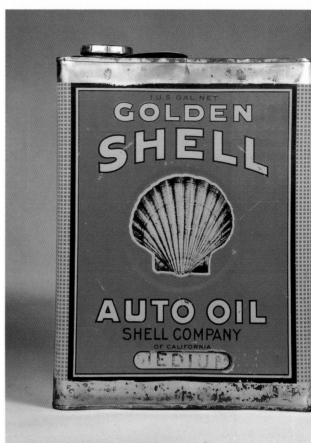

Golden Shell Auto Oil, $650 - 800

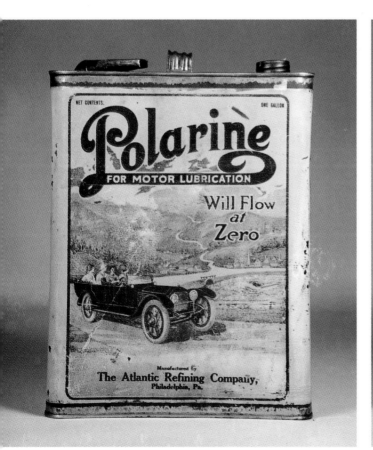

Polarine Motor Lubrication (Atlantic Refining Company), $325 - 450

Pioneer Oil, $45 - 65

Shell Motor Oil, $275 - 300

Independent Motor Oil, $150 - 200

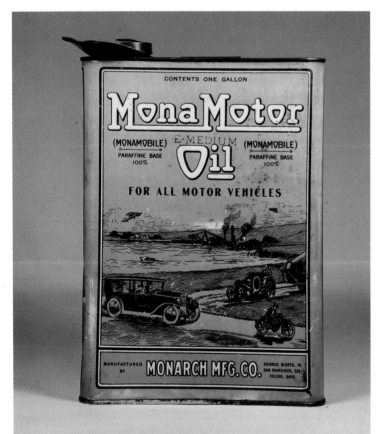

Mona Motor Oil, $325 - 475

Power-lube Motor Oil, $1200 - 1450

French Auto Oil, $850 - 1000

En-Ar-Co Motor Oil, $40 - 70

Conoco Motor Oil, $700 - 950

Penreco Motor Oil, $80 - 90

The Pep Boys 600 Transmission, $250 - 285

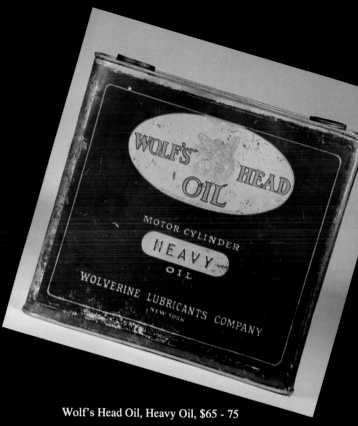

Wolf's Head Oil, Heavy Oil, $65 - 75

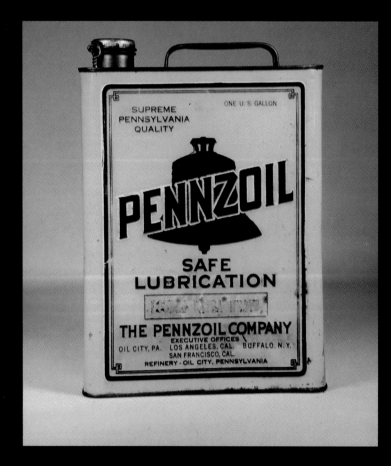

Pennzoil Safe Lubrication, $80 - 95

Trop-Artic Auto Oil, $950 - 1400

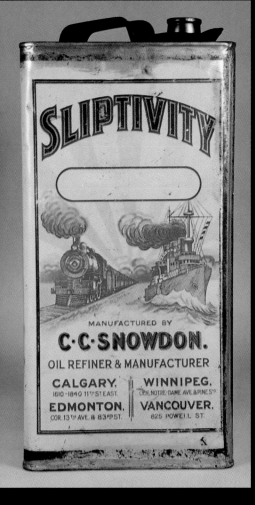

Havoline Oil, $140 - 150

Sliptivity (Canadian), $275 - 325

Lilly White Petroleum, $900 - 1 000

American Packard High Grade (Canadian), $375 - 400

Marathon Motor Oil, $100 - 1 10

Galenol Motor Oil, $40 - 65

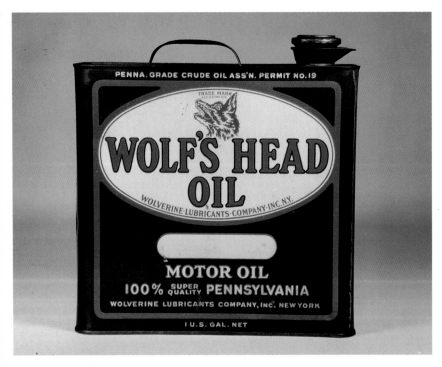

Wolf's Head Oil, $65 - 75

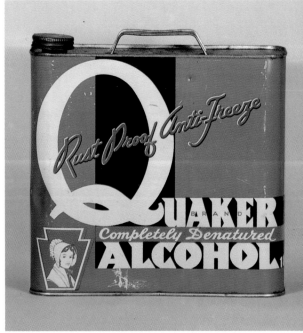

Quaker Alcohol, Rust Proof Anti-Freeze, $40 - 50

Amalie Motor Oil, $40 - 65

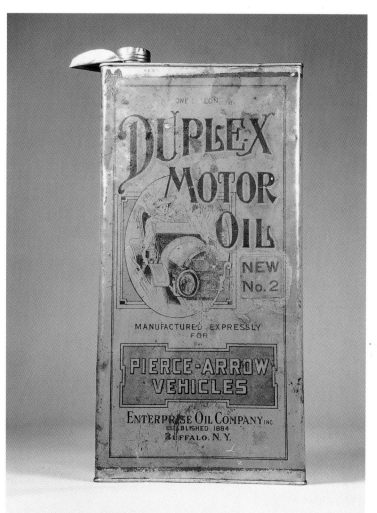

Duplex Motor Oil, $65 - 90

Russolene Pure Pennsylvania Motor Oil, $90 - 110

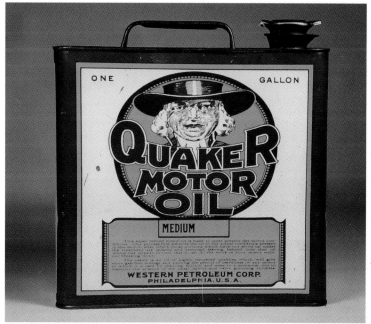

Quaker Motor Oil, $150 -225

Quaker State Medium Heavy Oil, $35 - 45

Quaker State Medium Oil, $30 - 40

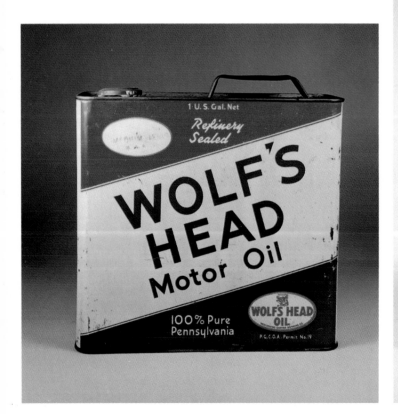

Wolf's Head Motor Oil, $30 -35

Excelsior Motor Oil, $750 -1000

Manhattan Automobile Cylinder Oil, $275 - 300

Caltex Multi-Purpose Thuban (Caltex is owned by Texaco), $55 - 75

Indian Oil, Indian Motorcycle Company, $750 - 1000

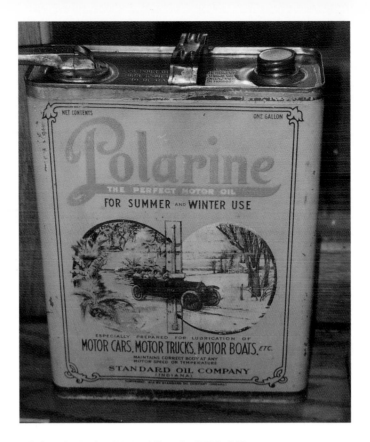

Polarine, the Perfect Motor Oil, early, $725 - 850

Atlantic Motor Oil can, $90 - 120

Texaco Gas Engine Oil, very early, $250 - 300
(Note 25 year watch on top)

F₅ CLASS F: HALF-GALLON OIL CANS

Tin half-gallon oil cans were in use from the early teens to the 1940s. Most of them were used by farms, factories, individuals and local filling stations.

McCormick-Deering Cream Separator Oil, $20 - 25

Keynoil Motor Oil, $250 - 325

Trop-Artic Auto Oil, $525 - 650

Penn Power Motor Oil, $125 - 150

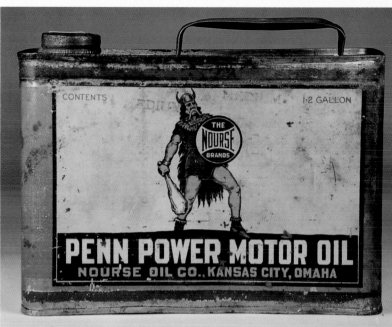

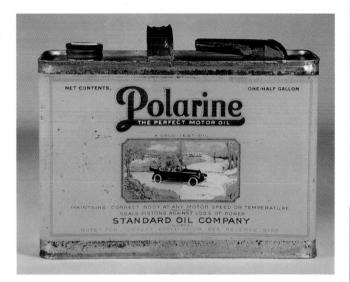

Polarine, the Perfect Motor Oil, $450 -675

Penn Star Motor Oil, $25 - 30

Empire Non Carbon Heavy Oil, $30 - 45

Pennelene Auto Oil, $40 - 50

Riverside Cream Separator Oil, $30 - 40

The Pure Oil Company Pure Oils, $70 -85

Lesh's Arkoline Products, $30 - 40

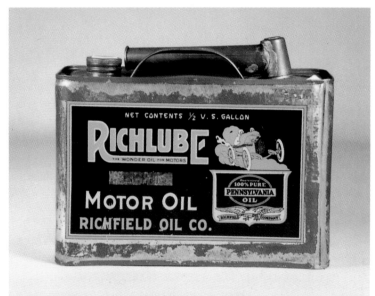

Richlube Motor Oil, $775 - 850

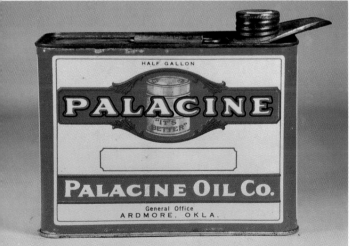

Palacine Oil, $130 - 150

Navy Motor Oil, $80 - 90

Goodell Auto Oil, $175 -185

Mona Motor Oil, $125 - 145

Sinclair Opaline Motor Oil, $120 - 135

Pierce Oil Corporation, Pennant Superior Quality, $40 - 55

Federal Oil Co., $170 - 195

Texaco Motor Oil, $145 - 155

Pennant, the Wonder Lubricant for Fords, $45 - 65

Conoco Harvester Oil, $650 - 800

Tagolene, Skelly Oil Company, $50 -70

Richlube Oils and Greases, $40 -55

Trop-Artic Auto Oil, $800 - 1350

Take a Spin with RED TOP Motor Oil, $275 - 325

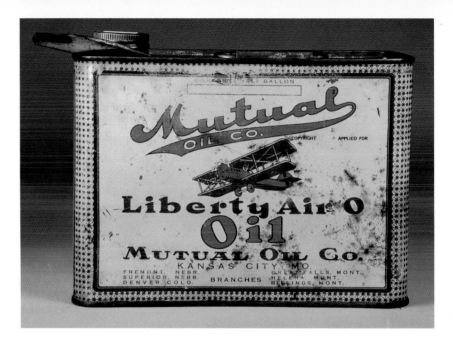

Mutual Oil Co., Liberty Air Oil, $190 - 240

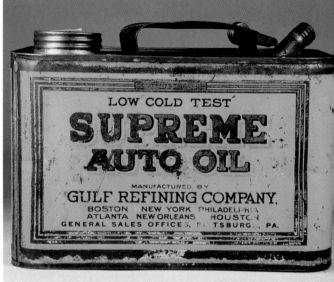

Supreme Auto Oil, Gulf Refining Company, $40 - 60

Pankey Motor Oil,
$40 - 50

Buffalo Oil and
Buffalo Harness Oil,
no pricing

CLASS G:
TIN FIVE-GALLON
ROUND OIL CONTAINERS

As advertised, these cans had an easy-pour spout and a handle for easy carrying. They were free standing.

Pennzoil Safe Lubrication can, $70 - 130

Marathon Motor Oil Transcontinental Oil Co. $175 - 250

Nourse Guaranteed Motor Oil, $250 - 300

HyVIS Motor Oil, $75 - 90

KOOLMOTOR OIL CITIES SERVICE, $70 - 90
Red Hat motor oil, $155 - 180
Marathon motor oil, $175-250

Penn Empire Motor Oil, $75 - 90

Coreco Motor Oil, $50 - 70

Arrow Motor Oil, $150 - 175

Tiger motor oil, $145 - 165
Keynoil White Eagle oil, $150 - 175
Bengol motor oil, $170 - 190

CLASS H:
TIN FIVE-QUART ROUND OIL CONTAINERS

These cans were used from the 1930s to the 1960s. Most of them were used in service stations and farms, and for home use.

Quaker State Medium Oil, $30 - 45

Tru-Penn, The Oilier Oil, $50 - 60

Oilzum Motor Oils and Lubricants, $120 - 135

Pennzoil Safe Lubrication, $85 - 90

Golden Shell Motor Oil, $60 - 70

Gargoyle Mobiloil, $95 - 100

Invader Motor Oil, $75 - 80

Harris Oils, America's Leading
Lubricants, $60 - 75

GulfLube Motor Oil, $40 - 50

Mileage Metered HyVIS Motor Oil, $35 -45

Kendall, the 2000 Mile Oil, $40 - 55

Veedol Motor Oil, $40 - 50

Gargoyle RED Band AERO
Mobiloil, $90 - 110

Sinclair Opaline Motor Oil, $50 - 60

Pennzoil Safe Lubrication,
"be oil wise," $90 - 100

"The Watchdog of Your Motor,"
Freedom Motor Oil, $70 - 80

CLASS I: ADVERTISING SIGNS

The following pictures show a variety of sizes and shapes of gasoline, motor oil, and related advertising signs. Most of these are porcelain, but some are painted tin. All are very colorful and very collectible.

Mobil Horse 4 foot, die cut, porcelain, $475 - 550

99 Mobiloel lubster sign from Germany, concave, porcelain, $275 - 325

Welch Guaranteed Motor Oil, $210 - 245

Pennzoil Expert Lubrication, $140 - 160

Sinclair Pennsylvania Motor Oil lubster sign, porcelain, $1250 - 1400

Texaco Star, die-cut, $50 - 65

Independent Quality Service, $275 - 330

Atlantic Motor Oil, Aviation tin, painted, $275 - 350

Welcome to our service department, Pennzoil tin, painted, $60 - 85

Bowes Expert Spark Plug Service tin, painted, flanged, $75 - 110

AC Spark Plugs tin, painted, $55 - 70

Quaker State Motor Oil two-sided, porcelain, $110 - 175

Mobil Flying Horse, die-cut, porcelain, $900 - 1200

Flying A, die-cut, porcelain, $150 - 175

Sales and Service Globe Battery Station, porcelain, $185 - 195

Mobil Flying Horse, 28" x 37", die-cut, porcelain, $600 - 775

Champion Spark Plugs tin, painted, $60 - 150

Kendall, the 2000 Mile Oil, painted, die-cut, $140 - 165

AJAX Cord Tires tin, painted, flanged, $140 - 175

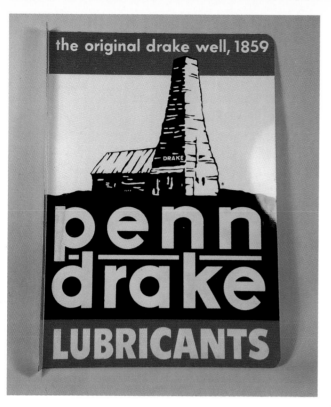

Penn Drake Lubricants tin, painted, flanged, no pricing available

Sinclair Opaline, small, porcelain, $400 - 600

Oilzum Motor Oils Lubricants, $200 - 300

Shell advertisement, paper, $40 -50

Shell, die-cut, raised letters, porcelain, $370 - 425

Magnolia Gasoline, two-sided, porcelain, $575 - 690

Bruinoil, Bruin Gasoline, die-cut, painted, flanged, $1600 - 1850

Pennzoil, We Are Bonded, one-sided, tin, $90 - 110

Supreme Pennsylvania Quality
Pennzoil, tin, $100 - 110

Phillips 66, die-cut for neon, $230 375

Mobil Flying Horse, 71" x 91", die-cut, porcelain,
$700 - 850

American AMOCO Gas Courtesy Cards Honored Here, two-sided,
porcelain, $80 - 110

Michelin, one-sided, porcelain, $220 - 275

Puritan motor oil, Stop Your Engine
Troubles, painted tin, $190 - 275

Phillips 66, two-sided, porcelain, $210 - 260

Mobil Flying Horse, die-cut, porcelain, 3', $625 -800

Penn-Drake motor oil tin, painted, embossed, $175 -220

Wolf's Head motor oil, flanged, painted tin, $65 -90

Sunray D - X, die-cut, porcelain, $475 - 600

MobiLubrication with horse, porcelain, fits on oil rack, $250 - 290

Mobil Flying Horse, 2', die-cut, porcelain, $1450 - 1575

Pennzoil Safe Lubrication, one-sided, porcelain, $325 -390

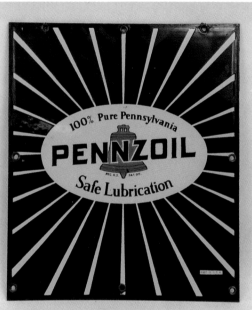

Pennzoil Lubrication, small, porcelain, $180 - 195

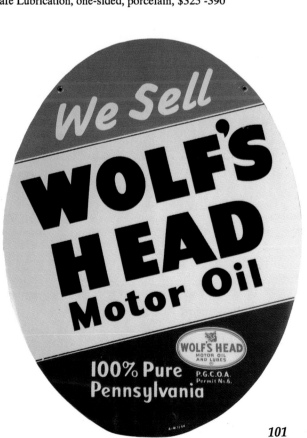

Wolf's Head motor oil, oval, painted tin, $55 - 95

OAK Motor Oil, one-sided, porcelain, $900 - 1 1 00

Mobiloil curb sign, porcelain, $275 - 300

Penn-Drake Motor Oil, die-cut, porcelain, $850 - 1100

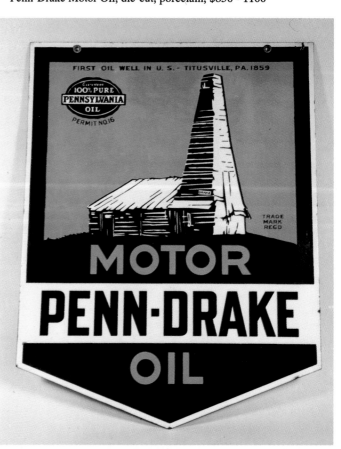

PennField Motor Oil curb sign, porcelain, $800 - 975

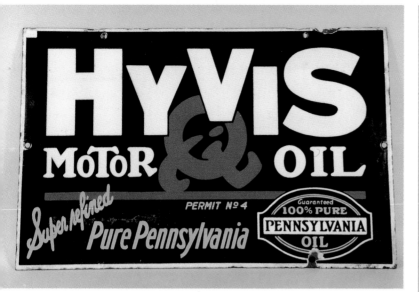

HYVIS Motor Oil, one-sided, porcelain, $225 - 260

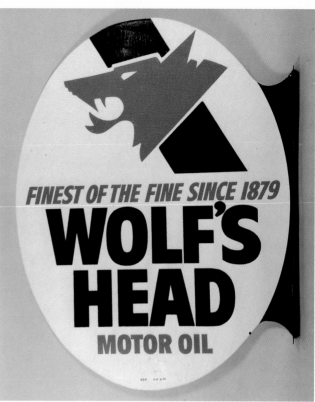

Wolf's Head Motor Oil, die-cut, flanged, tin, painted, $50 - 65

We Sell U VICO Oils and Greases, porcelain, $50 - 95

Hood Tire Dealer, 3' high, die-cut, porcelain, $2000 - 2500

More Power, More Speed, Champion Spark Plugs, tin, painted, embossed, $110 - 140

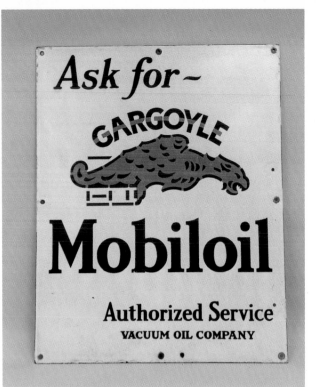

Sinclair Opaline Motor Oil, one-sided, porcelain, $150 - 175

Gargoyle Mobiloil Vacuum Oil Company, one-sided, porcelain, $255 -280

Sinclair Oils lubster sign, small, porcelain, $325 - 415

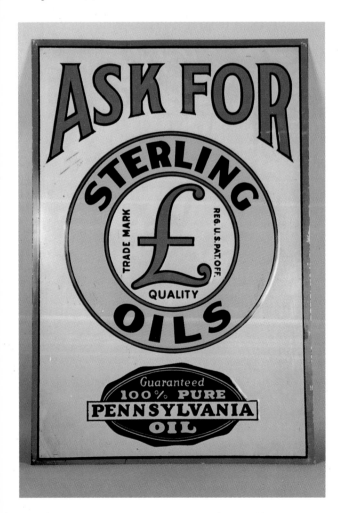

ASK FOR Sterling Oils, tin, painted, $120 - 135

Gargoyle Mobiloil, early, porcelain, $325 - 400

More and Cheaper Miles EMPIRE Motor Oil, cardboard, self-framed, tin, $195 - 250

Bonded Pennzoil Dealer, Pennzoil Safe Lubricatiorl, small, two-sided, tin, painted, $40 - 70

Penn Empire, More Miles, Less Cost, cardboard, self-framed in tin, $195 -145

Kendall, the 2000 Mile Oil, 30" x 20", large, die-cut, porcelain, $400 -525

Carabao Petroleum, The Texaco Company, two-sided, porcelain, flanged, $850 - 1200

United Motors service, two-sided, porcelain, $800 - 950

Amalie Motor Oil curb sign, porcelain, $140 - 170

SOCONY - VACUUM Aviation Products unusual, early, $575 - 700

Havoline Oil, "It makes a difference," early, one-sided, porcelain, $220 - 270

Havoline, early, porcelain, $155 - 175

Texaco, Hiule Pour Autos (France), two-sided, porcelain, flanged, $700 -950

Husky Service, two-sided, die-cut, porcelain, $1450 - 1800

Blue Grass Axle Grease, tin, painted, pre-automobile, $275 - 325

Power-Lube Motor Oil, two-sided, porcelain, $950 - 1200

Sinclair, "This Crop Grown With," tin, painted, $250 - 325

Texaco Mail Port, one-sided, porcelain, $475 - 650

Seaside Gasoline, $145-170

New Era Motor Oils Gasoline, round, porcelain, no pricing available

108

Bolene Blue Seal Gasolene, porcelain,

Sunoco A to Z Lubrication, die-cut, tin, $400 - 450

Harbor Petroleum Products, porcelain, $3600 -4800

Grizzly Gasoline, die-cut, very rare, $1150 - 1600

Union 76 car service sign, two-sided, porcelain, $190 - 230

Flying Horse, small, die-cut for neon, porcelain,
$700 - 850

Sinclair Oils, early, porcelain, $195 - 250

Conoco Superior Gasoline, very rare, porcelain, $2300 - 2600

Time Gasoline, large, porcelain, $175 -250

Marathon Products curb sign, two-sided, porcelain, $875 - 950

Standard Oil Co. gasoline price sign, very early, porcelain, $2200 - 2800

Marathon, Best In The Long Run, large, painted tin, early, $390 -475

111

Mohawk Gasoline, neon sign, no pricing available

Sunray DX Petroleum Products, two-sided, porcelain, $475-525

Red Crown Gasoline flanged, porcelain 275 - 325

Red Crown Gasoline, Standard Oil Company, early, $350 - 375

FISK, embossed, painted, tin, no price available

No-Nox GULF Motor Fuel, early, flanged, porcelain, $175 - 250

Marfak Lubrication, large, tin, painted, $80 - 125

Cities Service Oils, large, two-sided, porcelain, $275 - 350

HOOD Tires, porcelain, $375 - 425
Purol Gasoline, two-sided, porcelain, $275 - 325

McColl-Frontenac Products, Red Indian, Canadian,
porcelain, $750 - 825

Shell Kerosene, rare, tin, painted, flanged, $300 - 375

Gargoyle Mobiloil curb sign, small, two-sided, porcelain, $375 -450

Havoline Motor Oil, large, tin, painted

Socony Air-Craft Oils, porcelain, $550 - 775

Colonial Lubrication Service sign, older, porcelain, $275 - 350

Mobiloil Marine curb sign, porcelain, $675 - 800

Phillips 66 curb sign, two-sided, porcelain, $275 - 300

Barnsdall Products, two-sided, porcelain, $225 - 350

Gasoline Phillips Motor Oils, two-sided, porcelain, $475 - 575

Conoco Gasoline, early, two-sided, porcelain, $2350 - 2600

Texaco Motor Spirit Motor Oil, Australian, small, two-sided, porcelain, $650 - 700

It's PURPLE, It's POWERFUL, early, cardboard and tin, $90 -120

United States Tires Are Good Tires, fold-out sign, $275 - 325

Recognized Servicenter AC Aircraft Products, tin, painted, $285 - 350

Zerolene Oils & Greases, die-cut, porcelain, flanged, $675 - 800

Golden Shell Motor Oil, die-cut, porcelain, $750 - 800

Authorized Service Gargoyle Mobiloil, die-cut, porcelain, $300 - 375

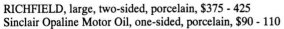

A nice display of a STERLING Oil sign.
no pricing available

RICHFIELD, large, two-sided, porcelain, $375 - 425
Sinclair Opaline Motor Oil, one-sided, porcelain, $90 - 110

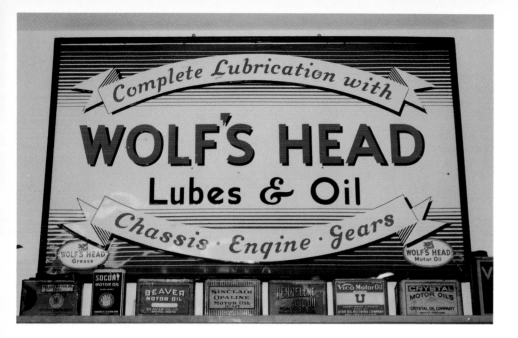

Wolf's Head Lubes & Oil, $175 - 230 (cans not included)

Conoco Germ Processed Motor Oils curb sign, two-sided, porcelain, $275 - 325

Higher COSDEN Octane, die-cut, no pricing available

Red Indian Motor Oils, one-sided, porcelain, $475 - 575

CALTEX, two-sided, porcelain, $550 -600

Perfect Circle Piston Rings, Piston Expanders, embossed, tin, painted, no pricing available

Gulfpride Marine H.D. porcelain, $400 - 450

TEXACO Motor Oil and TEXACO Motor Spirit, two-sided, porcelain, flanged, $550 - 675

Texaco no smoking sign, porcelain, $1550 -2000

Ace High Motor Oil curb sign, porcelain, $3200 - 3600

Deep Rock painted two-sided Air Race Premium 475 - 550.

Havoline motor oil, die-cut, porcelain, $675 - 800

Texaco Marine Lubricants, porcelain, $1650 - 2200

Kendall, the 2000 Mile Oil, die-cut, porcelain, no pricing available

Magnolia Petroleum, two-sided, porcelain, $550 - 675

White Star, two-sided, porcelain, $190 -250

Beacon oil, two-sided, porcelain, $475 - 550

Esso Imperial Products, one-sided, porcelain, $160 - 180

Texaco Gasoline Motor Oil, two-sided, porcelain, $450 - 500

Esso Aviation Products curb sign, porcelain, $550 - 675

Gulf Supreme Motor Oil one-sided porcelain 650 - 750

Gulf, two-sided, porcelain, $300 - 375

Mobilgas with gargoyle, one-sided, porcelain, $475 - 600

Texaco motor oil, one-sided, porcelain, $525 - 675

Texaco Filling Station, 1915, one-sided, porcelain, $1650 - 2000

Nourse motor oil, two-sided, porcelain, $675 - 750

CLASS J:
THERMOMETERS

The following pictures are of a variety of oil company advertising therometers. They were made of tin, wood, and porcelain.

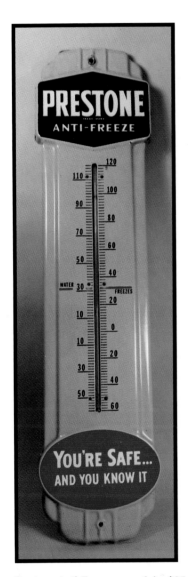

Prestone Anti-Freeze, porcelain, $85 - 110

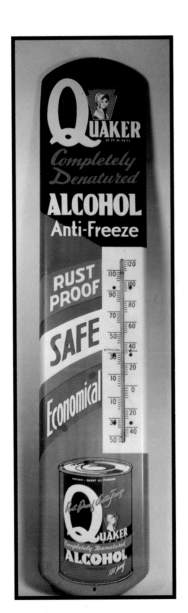

Quaker Alcohol Anti-Freeze, colorful painted tin, $300 - 325

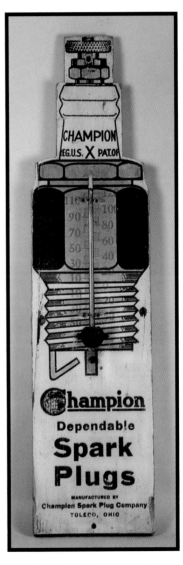

Champion Spark Plugs, die-cut, wooden, $185 - 260

Five Star Anti-Freeze, tin, painted, $60 - 90
Shellzone Anti-Freeze, tin, painted, $90 - 110

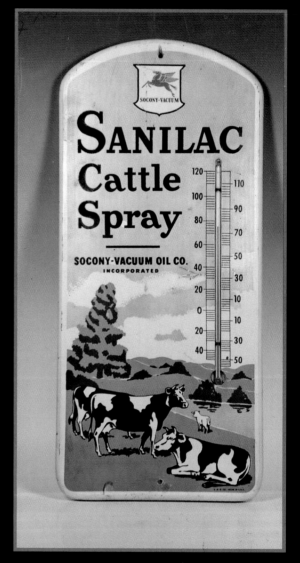

Sanilac Cattle Spray, tin, painted, $360 - 400

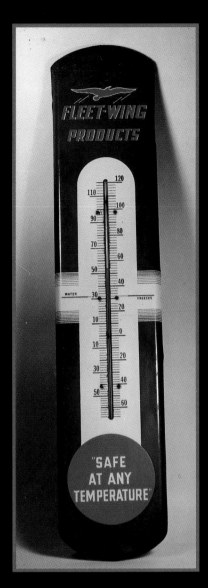

Fleet-Wing Products, tin, painted, $80 -95

Mobilgas Friendly Service Thermometer, $400 - 500

Mobil Socony Friendly Service, porcelain, $450 - 575

CLASS K:
PUMP PLATE SIGNS

The following pump-plate signs met motorists at their appropriate stations. Each sign was att.ached to a gas pump, announcing to the driver its brand and whether the driver would get Regular or Ethyl gasoline. Most of these signs were porcelain, but a small percent were painted tin.

Curt's Power Packed Regular, tin, painted, $60 - 90

Flying A, small, porcelain, $270 - 325

Curt's Power Packed Ethyl, tin, painted, $60 - 90

Texaco, 10", one-sided, porcelain, $225 - 275

Golden West Oil Company,
small, porcelain, $295 - 380

Sky Ranger, small, porcelain, $1100 - 1500

Gulf Dieselect Fuel, porcelain, $250 -340

Sunoco Motor Oil, small, porcelain, $350-375

Sinclair H-C Gasoline, porcelain, $450 - 550

Gulf Dieselect, small, porcelain, $45-60

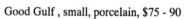

Good Gulf , small, porcelain, $75 - 90

Sky Chief Texaco Gasoline, porcelain, $95 - 130

Indian Gasoline, small,
porcelain, $225-275

Shell Gasoline, porcelain, $675 - 750

Golden Eagle, porcelain, 250 - 300

Sterling Ethyl Gasoline, small, porcelain, $450 - 500

Atlantic Hi-Arc, porcelain, $90 - 110

Gulf Super Marine, porcelain, $120 - 150

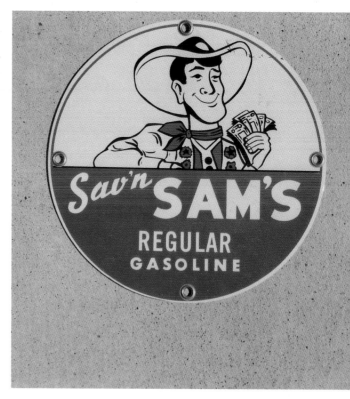

Sav'n Sam's Regular Gasoline, small, porcelain, $250 - 375

Atlantic Kerosene, porcelain, $120 - 130

United Hi-Spirit, early, porcelain, $350 - 375

Shamrock Cloud Master, small, porcelain, $65 - 90

Shell Premium Gasoline, porcelain, $750 - 850

Flying A Gasoline, small, porcelain, $175 - 225

Atlantic White Flash, small, porcelain, $110 - 130

Moore's Ethyl Supreme, porcelain, $175 - 200
Moore's Regular Supreme, porcelain, $175 - 200

Diesel Chief, small, tin, painted, $175 - 225

Sinclair Pennsylvania Motor Oil, porcelain, $475 - 650

Texaco, very early, large curved, porcelain,
for a fry pump, $350-475

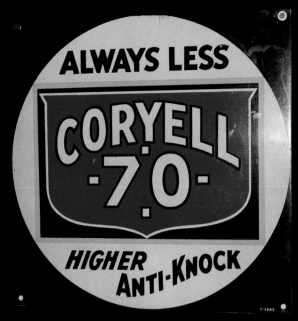

CORYELL, no pricing

Sky Chief Gasoline, small, porcelain, $125 - 150

Sky Chief Su-preme Gasoline, small, porcelain, $150 - 190

Super Gloco Ethyl, porcelain, $140 - 165

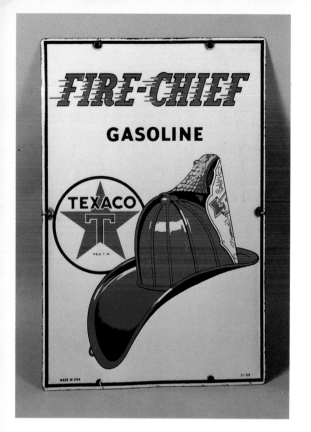

Fire-Chief Gasoline, $80 - 115

Texaco Diesel Chief, porcelain, $125 - 145

Blue Sunoco, die-cut, porcelain, $135 - 180

Sinclair Opaline Motor Oil, porcelain, $475 - 650

Cities Service Oils, porcelain, $170 - 195

Beacon Oils, die-cut, porcelain, $215 - 245

Mobilfuel Diesel, porcelain, $250 - 300

Texaco, for a Fry pump, early, curved, porcelain,
$550 - 575

Sky Chief Gasoline, porcelain, $185 - 200

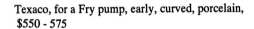

Texaco Marine White Gasoline, rare,
curved, porcelain, $1400 -1550

Conoco, early, porcelain, $475 - 525

Humble Continuously Improved, porcelain, $90 - 110

Higher COSDEN Octane, porcelain, $250 - 275

Whitlock Super Gasoline, porcelain, $425 - 475

Mobilgas Special, porcelain, $140 - 160

Sinclair Gasoline, porcelain, $40 - 60

Atlantic Diesel Fuel, small, porcelain, $125 - 150

Blue Sunoco 200 X, porcelain, $135-180

INDEX